Family Means...

Written by Matthew Ralph

Illustrated by Badrus Soleh

All families are different.

What does family mean to you?

Family means...

making silly faces.

Family means...

enjoying mealtimes.

Family means...

going on
adventures.

Family means...

working as a team.

Family means...

sharing with others.

Family means...

Family means...

playing in the dirt together.

Family means...

taking care of each other.

Family means...

putting a smile on someone's face.

Family means...

learning from one another.

But most of all...
Family means...

spending time with
the people you love.

Now it's your turn...
Write your own page.

Family means...

···

···

Draw your family.

About the author

Matthew Ralph is a children's book author who lives in London, England.

When he is not busy writing his next book, he enjoys drinking tea, eating fish & chips and waving at The Queen.

Matthew always enjoys hearing from his lovely readers as well as reading your comments. If you liked this book, please leave a review!

If you would like to learn more about him, visit his website:

www.mattralphthewriter.com

Get a FREE sloth-themed Digital Activity Book based on Matthew's best-selling book "Sam The Speedy Sloth."

The activity book includes coloring pages, spot the difference, word searches and a fun rainforest quiz!

Sign up to Matthew's newsletter to get this FREE activity book as well as news, updates and exclusive discounts:

www.mattralphthewriter.com/sign-up

More books by Matthew Ralph

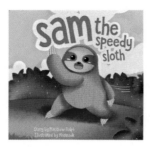

Sam The Speedy Sloth

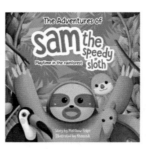

The Adventures of Sam The
Speedy Sloth:
Playtime in the rainforest

Gia The Not Giant Giraffe

Personalized Sloth Book

Personalized Giraffe Book

ABC Animal Facts

Go On... Press It

Spot The Difference

A Knightess In Shiny Armor

www.mattralphthewriter.com

Made in the USA
Middletown, DE
23 October 2021